DOLLS, TOYS & GAMES

ANTIQUES ROADSHOW
— POCKET GUIDE —

DOLLS, TOYS
&
GAMES

HILARY KAY

BBC BOOKS

A MARSHALL EDITION

Published by BBC Books, a division of BBC Enterprises Ltd,
Woodlands, 80 Wood Lane, London W12 0TT

Conceived, edited and designed by
Marshall Editions
170 Piccadilly, London W1V 9DD

ISBN 0 563 37130 7

10 9 8 7 6 5 4 3 2 1

EDITORS GWEN RIGBY, HEATHER MAGRILL
ART EDITOR HELEN SPENCER
PICTURE EDITOR ELIZABETH LOVING
ASSISTANT EDITOR SIMON BEECROFT
ART DIRECTOR JOHN BIGG

ILLUSTRATIONS by János Márffy, Coral Mula
ALL PHOTOGRAPHS by Clive Corless

Valuation is an imprecise art and prices vary for
many reasons. The valuations given are estimated
auction prices at the time of going to press.
As auctions take place in the public arena, this
is considered to be the fairest value.

Origination by Master Image, Singapore
Type film by Dorchester Typesetting
Printed and bound in Portugal by Printer Portuguesa

CONTENTS

INTRODUCTION

MADE TO LOVE, ENTERTAIN OR EDUCATE, TOYS have formed a part of everybody's childhood. All of us recognize with delight the toys from our own era. Some of us still carefully tend the dolls played with by our mothers and grandmothers, others wish we could find the doll of which such fond memories remain. It is understandable, then, that toys and dolls are so widely collected today, their shapes and faces stirring such deep memories within us.

The development of toys is linked closely to society's changing attitude toward children. Until the 18th century, children were regarded merely as small, naive adults. Children from aristocratic families were expected to amuse themselves as adults did, and miniature suits of armour and swords, for example, were provided for their entertainment. Children from the lower social orders were, of course, put to work at an early age, and their amusements would have been limited to whatever could be found; often this may have been nothing more than an inflated pig's bladder, which would have been patted about like today's balloons.

In the 18th century, the first books were produced commercially for children and it was discovered that a child could learn through play. Toward the end of the century, printed educational games and puzzles became available, which would, no doubt, have been sold in William Hamley's London toy shop, opened in 1760. Carved wooden toys such as tops, balls and Noah's arks were produced in southern Germany and were exported widely.

The Industrial Revolution created mechanized and inexpensive production techniques and led to machine-made toys of tin-plated sheet steel. Alongside this industrial growth was the emergence of the middle class, with enough money to demand machine-made toys and dolls for their children: the toy and doll industry was born.

Children 100 years ago were tempted by an enormous variety of toys: dolls with heads of porcelain, wax or papier mâché; wooden dolls' houses filled with painted tin-plate furniture; soft stuffed animals; the first toy railway; tin-plate and hand-painted vehicles and boats; and hollow-cast lead soldiers.

Toys were produced in great numbers between 1910 and the 1930s. Designers were quick to replicate real life in miniature and factories accurately reproduced each new technical advance: flying machines, submarines, underground railways and battle tanks. It is from this period that the earliest living memories date: of the streamlined saloon car with a clockwork motor, the pugnacious green tank locomotive, the golden teddy bear. But another toy first seen in the 1930s gained a huge audience of children worldwide – the Dinky Toy.

Produced in the first instance simply as accessories to enhance Hornby's railway layouts, Dinky Toys could be bought with pocket money and were up-to-the-minute designs of vehicles which any child might see any day in their own town. Toys at last were produced for the masses at affordable prices, and this concept has largely remained with manufacturers ever since.

Dolls
&
Soft Toys

Happy childhood memories of a
beloved doll or teddy draw many people
into collecting toys. Often charming, these
objects have now become very popular
and can prove to be valuable.
The best pieces, such as 18th-century
wooden dolls with their original clothes
or early Steiff teddy bears in perfect
condition, can fetch remarkably high
prices at auction. Over recent years,
the popularity of this field has
increased to the extent that almost any
prewar toy in good condition will attract
a collector. As with all antiques, the
most important consideration for
the buyer is the state of repair; although
well-loved but damaged toys may
be very appealing, they are
generally less valuable.

IDENTIFYING DOLLS

Many clues to a doll's age and origin are provided by the materials from which it is made, its body composition and shape. One of the most common types of old doll found today dates from 1915–25. They have bisque heads, with any makers' marks incised on the back.

These may be partly hidden, but by carefully easing up the wig at the back of the neck to expose the details, and by refer-ring to a book on doll trade-marks, amateurs can quite easily interpret the symbols.

For instance, those shown in **6** below can be deciphered as "F.S. & Co." (Franz Schmidt & Co.); "1272" (the mould refer-ence number, used *c*.1910); "58" (code for the size). "Deponiert" means that the maker claims registration. This information enables the doll to be quite accurately dated and valued.

DOLLS' HEADS

China heads, necks and shoulders (**1**, **2**), popular in 1840–70, were usually German. Bisque heads (**3**) were common by the end of the 1880s. Eyes were made of glass in wax dolls (**4**) and bisque dolls; in the pressed felt dolls of the 1920s (**5**) they could be either glass or painted. Bisque dolls from the 1880s onward (**6**) usually bear makers' marks on the back of the head.

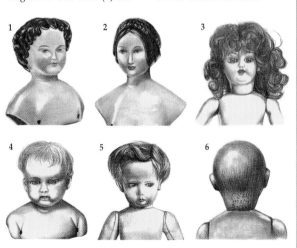

▽ **THREE DOLLS** *Until 1800, dolls were usually made of cloth, wood or wax, with the legs of most wooden dolls peg-jointed at the hip and knee. From 1800 to the 1870s, bodies tended to be made of shaped and padded kid or cloth, gusseted and seamed so they could be realistically posed. Bodies made of paper and wood pulp (1), with ball joints at hip, knee, shoulder and elbow, were used with bisque heads from the late 1870s. Bisque heads and composition "toddler bodies" (2), with curved limbs jointed only at the shoulder and hip, became popular after 1909. In 1900–20, celluloid (3) was used as a cheap alternative to bisque and composition; another cheap material was felt (see 2 below).*

DOLLS' LIMBS

The limbs of early wooden dolls were made separately and slotted in. Early padded or kid dolls did not have articulated joints, but by the 1880s jointed composition bodies were common. Hands of kid stuffed with kapok (1) can be found on china and bisque shoulder dolls after c.1860. The 1920s felt doll (2) has stitched and padded hands, and the arms are jointed only at the shoulder.

NON-BISQUE DOLLS

The earliest dolls in many collections are wooden, with the head and body turned from a single piece of wood and the legs slotted into the bottom of the body; they date from the 1730s. Because their limbs are pegged together to allow movement, they are sometimes known as "peg" dolls.

The head, chest, lower arms and legs of wooden dolls are generally covered with gesso – a type of plaster – and then painted to resemble flesh. Originally the eyes were also painted, but in the 1700s black enamel eyes were inserted into the head to make them appear more lifelike.

By the 1830s, dolls made of papier mâché, which could be moulded by machine, were being produced in large numbers in Germany and exported all over Europe. Wax, too, which can be easily shaped, was used in several ways to make dolls' heads or "shoulder heads", where the head and shoulders were cast together.

Wax gives the most natural-looking features, but it is soft, difficult to work with and expensive, so it was a long time before it was deemed to be suitable for mere toys.

▷ GEORGE III
WOODEN DOLL *This*
unusual English doll
has rouged cheeks,
inserted black eyes
without pupils,
feathered brows and a
blonde wig. Her waist
is tapered to rounded hips,
her legs end in block feet, and she
has wooden forearms, with long,
bent fingers. c.1790; 13½in tall.
£800–£1,200

▽ **PAPIER MÂCHÉ DOLLS** The 18½-inch standing doll is a papier mâché shoulder head doll, whose dark, plaited wig hides a black-painted head. She was made in Germany c.1850. **£500–£700**
The unusually tall seated doll measures 27 inches. She was also made in Germany – at the end of the 19th century – and has two moulded lower teeth, fixed blue glass eyes and a mohair wig. **£300–£500**

▷ **WAXED-COMPOSITION SHOULDER HEAD DOLL** with a cloth body and wooden lower arms. She has fixed glass eyes and a wig made from real hair. Her mouth is open and she has both upper and lower teeth. She still wears her original clothes. c.1865; 19in tall. **£300–£500**

WAX DOLLS

The heyday of wax-doll making was from the early 1800s to the 1930s. The wax used was beeswax, bleached, coloured and strengthened with additives. Dolls are of three types: solid wax (these tend to be older and smaller and are rarer), poured wax and wax over composition or papier mâché.

The main drawback to wax over composition is that the thin layer of wax expands and contracts at a different rate from the composition and so is prone to cracking, which does affect the value.

Eyes and hair varied according to the type of doll. The eyes of a solid wax doll were painted on or were glass attached by molten wax. Most poured wax dolls had proper eye sockets, with glass eyes attached to the inside of the head. The heads of wax over composition dolls were strong enough to take the weight of eyes that opened and closed, which were also fixed inside the head.

The simplest hair was carved or moulded; wigs were made by attaching human hair or mohair to a cloth base. Sometimes hair was inserted into small slits all over the head and the slits resealed. Some wax over composition dolls had a clump of hair inserted into a single large slit on top of the head.

◁ **ENGLISH POURED WAX DOLL** *with wax lower arms and legs, a cloth body and hair inserted into the head in clumps. The brown stain on her face is the result of ageing. She still has her original clothes and bonnet. c.1880; 16in tall.*
£400–£600

△ **WAXED-COMPOSITION DOLLS** *These German slit-head dolls have mohair ringlets, cloth bodies and kid forearms. Such pairs with similar or matching clothes are extremely unusual. c.1840; 21in tall.* **The pair £500–£700**

CLOTH AND KID BODIES

Most wax dolls have kid or cloth bodies. They were made in sections, of calico stuffed with cow hair or sawdust, and were then stitched together. The wax head and shoulders were always made as one piece, with holes at the back and front (often reinforced with metal eyelets) so that they could be stitched to the torso.

In the 1850s, the German maker Charles Motschmann patented "floating" limbs, in which the upper arms, upper legs and midriff were made from unstuffed cloth tubes.

▽ **CLOTH BODIES WITH LITTLE SHAPE** *tended to be used for baby dolls. Like most wax dolls, the head, lower legs and lower arms were of wax over composition.*

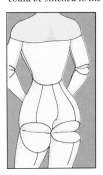

◁ **KID WAS OFTEN USED** *to model the curavceaous shapes of French fashion dolls. Gussets were used on kid bodies at elbows and knees to allow more realistic posing of the limbs.*

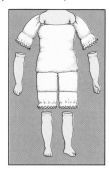

FRENCH BISQUE DOLLS

During the 18th century, France gained a reputation for fine-quality dolls, but by the early 1800s the French faced fierce competition from English wax dolls and, after 1830, from papier mâché dolls that were mass produced in Germany.

After 1840, several French makers, including companies such as Jumeau, Gaultier and Bru began producing bisque dolls of great beauty (in 1842, 1860 and 1866 respectively).

Two types of doll were commonly made: the bébé and the lady doll, or Parisienne, whose golden age was the 1860s and 1870s. These lady dolls usually have a bisque shoulder head

▷ JUMEAU FASHION DOLL
Such dolls as this bisque Parisienne with a swivel head are highly prized by collectors. She has a closed mouth, fixed blue eyes and a blonde mohair wig over a cork pate. Her body is leather, with separately stitched fingers, and she is dressed in the height of fashion in a finely embroidered cream on beige silk taffeta dress with a matching hat, leather shoes and silk stockings.
c.1875; 18in tall.
£4,000–£5,000

stitched on to a kid body, with the lower arms and legs often made of porcelain.

The high-quality bisque heads usually have large and lustrous blown-glass eyes, which gives them a particularly lifelike quality. The mouths are closed, the ears are often pierced, with earrings, and the dolls have real hair or mohair wigs in an elaborate coiffure.

The Parisiennes were finely dressed dolls seen not only as playthings but also as models for the latest French fashions.

▷ "MADAME BARROIS"
A swivel-head lady doll with fixed blue glass eyes, pierced ears and a blonde mohair wig over a cork pate. She has a gusseted kid body, her fingers are separately stitched and she is wearing her original silk gown with a bustle and brown button boots. c.1852; 15in tall. **£2,500–£3,500**

▷ BÉBÉ DOLLS *were made to represent small children. Their bodies are usually wood and composition with eight joints and straight wrists, as with this Jumeau doll. She has fixed blue glass eyes, applied pierced ears and a brown mohair wig over a cork pate. Her dress and shoes are not original. 1875; 23in tall.* **£2,000–£3,000**

GERMAN BISQUE DOLLS

For about 90 years, from the mid-1800s, the most popular material for dolls' heads was bisque – a once-fired, unglazed porcelain made from kaolin, which gave a matt finish. A plentiful supply of kaolin and a large, poorly paid workforce in Germany ensured that, between 1870 and 1940, millions of bisque dolls were made there and exported all over the world.

Early dolls had moulded hair and fixed glass eyes. Later, the heads were tinted in flesh tones, and the dolls were given mohair or real hair wigs and gravity-operated "sleeping" eyes.

Dolls' bodies were mainly papier mâché, although some were made of bisque and these are known as "all bisque" dolls. As is common elsewhere, the

◁ **EARLY BISQUE DOLL**
made by Simon & Halbig. The company started in 1870, but this unmarked shoulder head doll was probably made later. She wears her original fine wool clothes, which have remained immaculate because the doll has been kept in a box. c.1880; 16in tall. **£400–£600**

TYPES OF MOUTH

1 Closed A small, slightly pursed mouth with a full lower lip found on early ceramic dolls.

2 Open Developed to give the face a more natural, smiling expression. The upper teeth and tongue may be visible.

3 Open/Closed A painted mouth which appears to be open but is not.

identification marks for maker, mould number and size are usually found either on the back of the doll's head or on the shoulder plate.

MAKERS OF BISQUE DOLLS
Armand Marseille; Bahr & Proschild; Gebrüder Heubach; Heubach Koppelsdorf; J.D. Kestner; Kammer & Reinhardt; Schoenau & Hoffmeister; Simon & Halbig

◁ **A CHARMING DOLL** *which has been given a new body and dress. She has a very good head, however, and is consequently valuable. She was made by the popular makers Gebrüder Heubach and bears the mould number 8192. c.1914; 12in tall.* **£150–250**

THE MOST EXPENSIVE DOLL IN THE WORLD

On February 8, 1994, a 25¼-inch bisque-headed doll was sold at Sotheby's in London, for the world record price of £190,000. She was made by Kammer & Reinhardt, mould no. 108, and is the only example discovered to date. It is possible that 108 was an experimental mould. It was modelled as a particular child with a wistful, half-smiling expression, very different to the faces of the majority of German bisque dolls seen today which were made in huge numbers. Character faces are generally more unusual and sought after.

△ **A DOLL**, *probably made by Simon & Halbig, with a toddler's body and the number 914 on the back of her head. Rather than the normal bland expression, she has what is described as a "character" face. c.1915; 14in tall.* **£250–£350**

DOLLS' FURNITURE

Most collector look for dolls' house furniture dating from the 1880s. There is no standard size for such furniture, and pieces from an inch to a foot in height are all classed as dolls' house, or miniature, furniture.

A variety of materials was used, including wood, metal, bone and tortoiseshell, and the detail is often superb. Types include carved bone items from India, Viennese gilt-metal pieces with enamel decoration and French pieces with carved wooden legs and silk upholstery. Wooden pieces painted with gold to simulate boulle inlay, from Walthershausen, Germany, are specially prized.

△ **THIS SECRETAIRE**, *made in Germany, shows a wealth of detail: it is decorated with gold scrollwork, the pigeonholes are flanked by two small cupboards, and three crowns ornament the cornice. c.1890; 6½in high.* **£250–£350**

▷ **DRESSING-TABLE MIRROR**
A beautifully made mirror in high-quality walnut with many period details including mouldings and bun feet. c.1880; 5in high. **£200–£300**

◁ **UPHOLSTERED CHAIR** *with a stained wood frame and turned legs. It is part of a set comprising armchairs, sofa (see bottom) and table, all ornately painted in gold scrollwork to resemble brass inlay. c.1880; 5in high.* **£50–£70**

▽ **WOOD-FRAME SOFA,** *upholstered in olive-green silk. The pale wood has been well carved and stained to resemble cherry. Originally there were four matching armchairs and a table. c.1890; 9in wide.* **£60–£80**

▷ **UPHOLSTERED SOFA** *in stained wood, with a carved back painted with gold scrollwork to resemble boulle. c.1880; 5in high.* **£50–£70**

Interest in collecting miniature furniture has grown over the past few years – whether for furnishing dolls' houses or for display. Even items made fairly recently, such as plastic furniture and crockery, have their own following with collectors.

A large number of functional items – kitchen equipment and china, for instance – are available, but decorative pieces, including hand-painted pictures in gilt-metal frames, are rarer and tend to fetch higher prices when they come to auction.

Articles that are hard to come by, such as birdcages, sewing machines and clocks, can command as much as £100 each.

DOLL'S PRAM

This piece is very closely modelled on the full-size perambulators which

would have been seen in Victorian cities in the 1890s. Made of painted wood with a padded interior, the pram has sprung suspension and is supported by delicate spoked wheels. Prams of this scale appeal to two groups of collectors: doll accessory collectors; and those who are interested in prams in their own right. 1890s. **£250–£300**

▷ **PINE TABLE** *stained to resemble oak. Although it was made in England, the legs are intricately carved in 17th-century Dutch style. The copper and aluminium jelly moulds are contemporary. c.1910; 4in high.* **£80–£120**

◁ **COUNTRY KITCHEN** *The table and chairs were made during World War II by a soldier serving in Burma; the pottery teapot, jugs and plate are from the same time. The other objects were all made in Germany in the 1890s. 5in high.* **£120–£200**

△ **MINIATURE FOOD TINS** *Made in Germany, this selection of containers for, among other things, cocoa, tea, salt and oats is transfer-printed in bright designs. c.1890; 2in high. The set* **£50–£70**

▽ **TIN-PLATE COOKING RANGE** *This is too big for a dolls' house and was probably meant as a toy for a child. The range is complete with methylated spirit heater, chimney with copper top, paw feet, a kettle and four cooking pots. c.1910; 13in wide.* **£200–£300**

TEDDY BEARS

Soft bears on all fours were made before 1900 and the first with movable joints in 1902, but it was not until 1906 that the teddy bear got its name.

Up to the 1920s, teddy bears looked fiercer than the cuddly teddies of today, for their features were modelled on the grizzly and brown bears. Until the 1930s, when bright scarlet, blue, purple and yellow bears appeared, their coats were natural in colour.

Initially, teddies were filled with excelsior (wood shavings) or a mixture of kapok and excelsior; later they were stuffed with kapok alone.

The best-known maker is the German company, Steiff. Other teddy-making firms include: Chad Valley, Merrythought and Pedigree in England; Schuco and Fleischmann & Bloedal in Germany; and the Ideal Novelty and Toy Company in the U.S.

△ **STEIFF BUTTONS** *Many of the most valuable bears were made by the German company Steiff, whose bears can be identified by a small metal button in the left ear. The design of the buttons has changed over the years and can, if they are in a good enough condition, be used for dating. Designs have included an elephant and the word "Steiff". Imitation buttons are now being made, so it may be useful to examine a genuine button before starting a collection.*

HOW TEDDY GOT HIS NAME

President Theodore "Teddy" Roosevelt was a keen hunter. In 1902 a cartoon appeared showing Roosevelt refusing to shoot a bear cub. The cartoon was well received and the bear cub was used in other cartoons of Roosevelt. At the same time, soft toy bears were being imported from Germany. They soon became popular with Roosevelt's adult followers and by 1906 the toys were known as "Teddy Bears".

◁ **STEIFF TEDDY** *Shown together with a photograph of his original owners, this fine gold plush teddy bear has the Steiff button in his ear. He has a humped back and is stuffed with excelsior. c.1908; 11in tall.* **£600–£800**

◁ **YES/NO TEDDY BY SCHUCO** *The tail of this gold bear is linked to his head – moving the tail turns the head from side to side and up and down. The loss of his ears, eyes and pads affects his value. 1925; 15in tall.* **£200–£300**

GUIDE FOR BUYERS

When collecting old teddy bears it is important to note that only those that can be identified as having been made by a particular firm and are in good condition are of any value.

▷ **GOLD PLUSH TEDDY** *This bear was made by Merrythought, an English toy-making company which was established in 1930 at Ironbridge in Shropshire. With his plastic nose, glass eyes and velvet pads with embroidered claws he is a good example of the well-made teddies Merrythought is known for. c.1950; 21in tall.* **£80–£120**

△▷ **SOMERSAULTING BEAR** *The unusual feature of this fine blond plush bear with his black boot-button eyes is his ability to turn somersaults. An internal mechanism means that when his arms are wound, he flips over. Made by the German firm Gebrüder Bing before World War I, this type of teddy is rare. c.1913; 13½in tall.* **£400–£600**

FEARSOME TEDDY

Over the last decade, teddy bears have become very popular with collectors. Although well-cuddled teddies are often the most endearing, they may be almost worthless. It is the bears in mint condition, and particularly those that are somewhat unusual, that are prized by collectors and fetch huge sums at auction.

This splendid 22-inch tall blond plush teddy is a fine example. He was made by Steiff, the most sought-after teddy maker, *c.*1908, has a brown stitched nose, a humped back and a growler in his stomach. He would fetch more than £5,000 at auction today.

▽ **MUSICAL BEAR** *Halfway down the back of this teddy is a key that winds up a mechanism operating a musical movement inside. Made by Schuco, a popular German toy maker, this teddy bear has gold plush "fur", black glass eyes, a hump back, a metal rod attaching the head to the body and swivelling joints. c.1925; 22in tall.* **£300–£500**

SOFT TOYS

Although some soft toys were made earlier, it was only in the 1890s that serious production of fabric animals and figures began.

They were generally made from felt, plush, velvet, printed cotton or fur cloth and were filled with kapok, excelsior (fine wood shavings), granulated cork and sometimes even sawdust.

Magarete Steiff, a German toy maker, was the first to make soft animals on a commercial scale. Still active today, her company is best known for its teddy bears, although it manufactured a variety of animals and dolls. All its toys were made of plush, felt

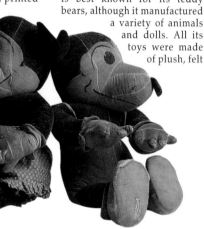

△ MICKEY AND MINNIE MOUSE *were both produced in England by Dean's Rag Book Company. Made of velvet and cotton, they are large and quite unusual. If they were in good condition, clean and with tails, their value could be twice as high. 1930s; 14in high seated.*
£600–£800

◁ **DOPEY** *This amusing velvet Dopey, with his painted face, was made for the promotion of Walt Disney's* Snow White and the Seven Dwarfs *in 1937. 10in high.*
£300–£400

◁ **SCHUCO BULLY BULLDOG** *is made from good orange and white plush. He has brown-tipped hair and is wearing a leather collar. The most popular animals for soft toys included dogs, cats, rabbits, lions, tigers, pigs and elephants. c.1927; 12in tall.* **£300–£400**

or mohair fur and marked with the distinctive Steiff button.

In the 1920s, another German firm, Schuco, began producing soft animals. These often had a clockwork movement or a wire link between the head and tail which turned the head as the tail was moved.

English factories also started to make soft toys: Dean's began production in 1903; Chad Valley and Norah Wellings in the 1920s; Merrythought in 1930 and Pedigree in 1942. The toys were marked by various means such as sewn-on labels, printed or woven tags, or names stencilled or stamped on the fabric.

The value of soft toys is particularly dependent upon their condition. Once badly stained or worn, they become almost impossible to repair.

△ **FELIX THE CAT** *The black-and-white plush cat on the right has felt ears, glass eyes and a humped back. His companion is made of felt and has a ribbon and squeaker. 1920s; 14in tall (right), 12in tall (left).* **Each £200–£300**

◁ **FELT ELEPHANT** *The four metal wheels allow this early Steiff toy to roll along. He also has a press squeaker in his belly. c.1897; 16in long.* **£350–£500**

TOY
FIGURES

Collecting toy figures, including such
diverse playthings as model soldiers,
space travellers and clockwork animals,
is becoming increasingly popular.
The term "antique toys" can be
misleading, since many are less than
100 years old. Indeed, most of the toys in
this section were made between the
1890s and 1940s, when factory
production became established.
Germany, America and Britain led the
world in manufacturing toy figures,
although many later examples, such
as the space toys which date mainly from
the 1950s and '60s, were made in Japan.
With the exception of some
lead soldiers, which can be expensive
and are much sought after, toy
figures, especially those made after
World War II, offer the new enthusiast
a relatively cheap and plentiful
source of collectables.

TOY SOLDIERS

Model soldiers have a long history, stretching back thousands of years. In ancient Egypt they were used to represent armies in the pharaohs' tombs, and Roman children are known to have played with figures of soldiers.

Solid and flat-cast lead soldiers have been popular for a few hundred years, but the mass production of lead alloy figures began only in 1893,

when the company William Britain & Sons perfected the hollow-cast method. Although makers such as Johillco and Reka Ltd. copied its methods, Britains was responsible for more than half the lead soldiers produced. It was only with the introduction of cheaper plastic figures in the 1960s that production diversified.

Although they are unmarked, the earliest figures from Britains,

△ ROYAL HORSE ARTILLERY "W" SERIES *Made by Britains, this set, no. 125, comes complete with its original box and is in good condition. Figures in the "W" series are smaller than standard size. c.1938; 2in high.* **£100–£120**

▷ MILITARY BAND FIGURES *The bugler in khaki dress was made by Johillco (John Hill & Co.), while the later drummer is from a nine-piece Britains set called "Bands of the Line". 1914–20; 2in high.* Each **£5–£8** (in mint condition **£10–£15**)

those with oval bases, can be identified by the high quality of the casting and painting. Great care was taken to ensure that uniforms, weapons and colours were correct. After 1900, paper labels were stuck to the bases to protect copyright, and from about 1905 cast lettering was used. Figures produced after 1907 had square bases.

The condition of toy soldiers is all-important, and an original box in good condition can double the price of a set. Beware of any damage or repainting which can significantly affect the value of a lead soldier.

△ **SOLID-CAST FIGURES** *These soldiers from the Napoleonic era include a standard-bearer, a fusilier and a mounted officer. They were all probably made by the Heyde factory in Dresden, Germany. 1895–1900; 2½in high.* Officer **£10–£15**; Infantry **£5–£10**

▽ **AN AMBULANCE WAGON** *of the Royal Army Medical Corps made by Britains, set no. 145. An earlier and more valuable version of this set is identifiable by its grey wagon, heavier collar harness and by flatter horses' ears. c.1924; 3½in high.* **£150–£200**

SPACE TOYS

When the first Sputnik satellite was launched in 1957, it heralded the beginning of the Space Age. This exciting new era not only influenced the design of cars and fabrics but also inspired the science fiction and space fantasy markets.

Comic strips featured such heroes as Buck Rogers and Dan Dare, and Hollywood made more films about space. The earliest space toys were actually produced as promotional spin-offs from these films. With the advent of television, more toys were inspired by programmes like *Space 1999* and *Fireball XL5*.

During the 1960s, the heyday of space toys, most were made

△ **MOON EXPLORER VEHICLE** *Both the rocket-shaped remote-control unit and the vehicle itself are in mint condition. It was made by Yonezawa and comes complete with lights, motor sound, moving antennae and its original box. 1960s; 8½in long.* **£120–£200**

by Japanese companies, usually of lithographed tin plate with plastic or Perspex detailing.

As this type of toy was made fairly recently and generally in large numbers, their condition is of paramount importance to the collector. High prices are only paid for toys in mint condition and preferably in their original boxes.

△ **MANOEUVRES IN SPACE** *These brightly coloured spacecraft were made by the Masudaya company. Their value is increased by the presence of the circling space walker. Such figures are rare since they have usually become detached over the years. 1960s; 8½in long (left).* Together **£200–£300**

◁ **TWO SPACECRAFT** *Both of these battery-powered toys have survived in excellent condition, a fact reflected in their value. The "Mars" spaceship (left), was made by Masudaya, while Yoshia made the spacerocket. 1960s; 14½in (left) and 13½in.* The pair **£250–£350**

ROBOTS & ASTRONAUTS

R̲ecent years have seen mechanical robot figures become popular collectables. These ingenious toys, inspired by the growing interest in space travel and science fiction since the 1950s, often now command high prices at auction.

Initially, Japan was the leading producer of toy robots. Companies such as Bandai, Linemar, Nomura and Alps

△ **PLASTIC DALEK** *A battery-powered model, available in silver or black, that was highly popular in the late '60s. A more accurate tin-plate version was made by Codeg. 6in high.* **£100–£150**

◁ **"DUX ROBOT ASTROMAN"** *Rare plastic figure made in Germany by Markes & Co. It is operated by a four-function remote control and the mechanism is visible inside its plastic chest. Late 1950s; 12in tall.* **£600–£700**

exported large numbers of tin-plate models in the 1950s and '60s, and plastic models from the '60s onward. Post-1960s battery-powered figures from Japan are highly collectable.

The best-known British robots are the Daleks, from BBC TV's *Doctor Who.* Although popular all over the world, most Dalek toys – both metal and plastic – were manufactured in Britain; those produced by Codeg during the 1960s are considered to be the finest.

New robots are generally battery powered and made of plastic. Tin-plate pieces, based on 1960s and '70s models from Japan and Europe, are still being made today in China and the former Soviet Union. Such items are a cheaper alternative to collecting older toy robots.

Before purchasing a battery-operated robot, remember to check for corrosion from acid leaks. The number of lights and moving parts does not affect value, and an original box is always a bonus.

◁ **RARE WALKING ROBOT ASTRONAUT** *The laser gun rises up to fire but the antenna on top of the helmet is missing. This tin-plate toy was made in Japan but, since its box is missing and it is unmarked, the maker is unknown. 1955; 10in tall.* **£300–£400**

▷ **TIN-PLATE "ROBOTANK Z"** *by Nomura of Tokyo. The eyes and the light between the two guns flash on and off, and the arms (each holding a lever) move, giving the effect of self-propulsion. 1960s; 10in tall.* **£100–£150**

ANIMAL TOYS

Noah's Arks are among the earliest wooden toys. Sometimes with more than 100 animals, they were highly popular in the 19th century. This type of toy was approved of by adults because of its religious associations.

With increased popularity of animal models as playthings, William Britain & Sons launched their lead farm animals in 1923. Farmyard accessories, zoo and circus animals followed. These detailed pieces are now fairly inexpensive to collect. Fox hunting sets were also produced.

When tin was introduced, lead toy making declined. Most tin-plate toys tend to be mechanical and are known as "novelty" pieces.

◁ **ELEPHANT "RINGMASTER"**
A celluloid clockwork elephant in a painted uniform and in such good condition is a rare find. 1920s; 7in high.
£150–£180

▽ **CAST-IRON HORSE AND CART**
Farmyard sets with accessories, such as haystacks and troughs, are particularly valuable. c.1900; 4in long. **£40–£60**

△ **WOODEN ELEPHANT**
This movable piece is from the "Humpty Dumpty Circus" made by the Schoenhut company. c.1925; 8in high. **£30–£40**

NOAH'S ARK

Bavaria was the most prolific producer of arks in Europe. Much sought after today, an early ark in good condition and containing around one hundred pairs of animals can fetch as much as £4,000. Flat-bottomed arks are not as collectable as the boat-shaped variety. This example, even complete with 72 figures is only worth £800.

An ark's animals and figures were individually hand-carved until the early 19th century, when they were sliced off a large carved ring of wood.

▽ *In the ring method a rough outline was carved into a block. When sliced, this produced animals of uniform size which were then finished by hand.*

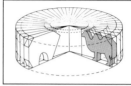

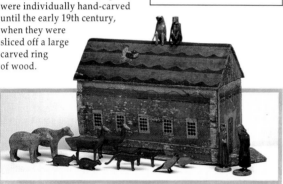

▽ **NOAH'S ARK FIGURES**
These models were made from Elastolin – a mixture of gum *arabic, chalk and sawdust – by the German company Elastolin. 1930s; 1in–6in high.* **£500**

AUTOMATA

When wound up, these mechanical amusements, known as automata, imitate the movement of a person or animal. They were essentially intended for adults, but of course also appealed to children.

The first true automata, incredibly intricate figures or animals with complex movements, were made in the 18th century. They were large and complicated, which made them expensive. In response to this, factories and workshops began to make smaller cheaper figures. Most of these were clockwork, although some later pieces were powered by electricity.

Fakes have recently appeared on the market and can be hard to spot. Check under the clothes to make sure the figure looks old and beware of tempting offers that seem too good to be true.

△ **MONKEY PLAYING THE FIDDLE**
Many of the best automata were made by French companies. This monkey, playing a fiddle in the garden of a chateau, was made by Phalibois. c.1875; 16in high.
£1,500–£2,000

◁ **"THE MARRIAGE PROPOSAL"** *This type of picture automaton was most commonly made in France. They reached the height of their popularity around the turn of the century.*

Once wound up, many parts of the scene are set in motion – figures pop up and down and eyes and limbs move. c.1900; 11in high. **£400–600**

▽ **Dancing Punchinello** *When the handle is turned, this amusing French-made doll dances while music plays from an internal movement. Hand-wound toys were originally cheaper than clockwork versions. c.1885; 11in high.*
£600–£900

△ **Nautical scene** *When set in motion the small doll on the shore waves at the ship being buffeted by heavy seas. c.1890; 16in high.*
£800–£1,200

▽ **Musical group** *These highly collectable figures were not made as a set. The pigs were marketed as "Walt Disney's Three Little Pigs". The girl conductor was made separately. c.1935; 5in high.* The group
£500–£700

NOVELTY TOYS

The term "novelty toys" encompasses a wide variety of pieces and includes amusing representations of figures from contemporary life and characters from films, fables and books.

Until the mid-20th century most of these tin-plate toys were both manufactured and sold in Europe. The most important toy makers of the time included: the big German manufacturers Märklin, Carette, Gunthermann, Bing and Plank, who are better known for their trains and road vehicles; other German toy makers Lehmann, Schuco, Adams and Stock; the French company Martin; and the American firm Marx.

△ CAT AND MOUSE TOY *Known as "Nina", this clockwork toy was made by Lehmann. The tin body has been painted and sprayed with a type of flock. It is unfortunate in terms of the value that the original box is not in better condition. 1920s; 7in long.* **£500–£600**

◁ GOOFY THE GARDENER *Disney characters, such as this one, are very popular with collectors. Goofy was made in both America and Britain by Louis Marx. 1935–40; 4in high.* **£150–£180**

The outbreak of World War II seriously disrupted the European toy-making industry, and when the Japanese started production, soon after 1945, they quickly became dominant.

In the 19th and early 20th centuries, most toys were powered by either a clockwork spring, a motor or steam. As this century has progressed, new forms of propulsion have been devised, including battery power, friction drive and gyroscopes.

▷ **TIN-PLATE BALLERINA**
A tiny gyroscope inside the foot of this fine German-made ballerina allows her to remain poised on one leg. 1950s; 5in tall. **£50–£80**

▽ **COCKEREL AND EGG CART** *This tin-plate clockwork toy was made by Lehmann in Germany and is known as the "Duo". Although it is scratched and the axle has been repaired, the piece is rare and is therefore still quite valuable. Lehmann was founded in 1881 in Brandenburg by Ernst Lehmann and is regarded as one of the best producers of novelty toys. 1930s; 6¾in long.* **£480–£550**

VEHICLES, TRAINS & CONSTRUCTION SETS

Model trains, cars, boats and
planes from earlier decades are hugely
popular with collectors. Since the
demand for these toys is high, many
enthusiasts specialize in collecting a
particular type, such as die-cast or tin-
plate vehicles; or a famous make,
such as Dinky model cars and
lorries or Hornby train sets.
Before World War I, production
was dominated by a small number of
German companies, including Märklin,
Bing and Carette, which exported
their toys around the world. The rarity
and quality of their pieces mean that
they are particularly valued by collectors.
The best prices are paid for scarce
items in "mint and boxed" condition,
that is, as they left the factory.

MODEL BOATS

Some of the most familiar types of model boat are the tin-plate variety. These water-going boats are powered by clockwork, steam or electricity. The most sought-after models are early 20th-century liners and battleships by such German toy makers as Bing, Carette, Märklin and Fleishmann.

Another important category of model boat is scale models of working vessels. They were made by skilled amateurs, often by sailors in their spare time, and range from simple fishing smacks to oil tankers. Intended for display rather than for use, some of the best examples of these wooden scale models are the finely detailed frigates and other war ships made by French prisoners during the Napoleonic Wars.

▽ **GUNBOAT** *The German company Carette, which made this tin-plate clockwork model, supplied the English company Bassett-Lowke with many of its models. In fact, this boat flies the Union Jack on both its masts. c.1904; 20in long.* **£600–£800**

△ **"LEVIATHAN"** *Tin-plate boats are prone to rusting, which means that well-preserved pieces are more valuable. This liner, made by Bing, is a fine example since its masts, propellors and paintwork are all intact. c.1920; 13in long.* **£400–£600**

Dinky's colourful "waterline" series of warships and liners made in the 1930s and '40s are a lesser category of collectable model boats. These small ships are distinguished by being keel-less and flat-bottomed.

Much rarer and more keenly desired are large-scale models of naval and merchant vessels professionally engineered by shipyard apprentices. Such models were typically presented to the shipyard owners and many are now on display in museums. Knowing the history of the ship represented is an added bonus for enthusiasts.

△ **"SS MASCOT"** *This remarkably detailed ship was constructed by an amateur, probably a member of the crew. The vessel's interior from wheelhouse to engine room is revealed layer by layer as the decks are removed. The details on each section are accurate and include buckets and a working compass. c.1910; 3ft 1in long.* **£1,000–£1,200**

◁ **BATTLESHIP** *made in tin plate by Bing. Pre-World War I German models, though never made to scale and often lacking detail, are highly sought after. Most are clockwork powered, but other examples, such as this, are driven by steam. c.1912; 30in long.* **£500–£700**

Tin-Plate Vehicles

Children's toys often mirror contemporary society. This is especially true of model vehicles. As modes of transport changed, so did the miniature versions made for children. Indeed, part of their fascination for collectors is as a memento of a world that has disappeared.

The first tin-plate vehicles were made in the early 19th century in Germany. They were generally cut out individually from large sheets of tin-plated steel, which were then shaped, soldered and painted by hand.

Around 1908, tin-plate toys began to be decorated using the offset lithography process. This involved printing both the design and the decoration on flat sheets of metal, which were then cut and shaped by machine. Small metal tabs were used to hold the toys together. This mechanization allowed the toys to be made in larger numbers and far more cheaply.

△ SMART SALOON CAR *Complete with battery-operated lights, a uniformed driver and doors and a boot that open, this clockwork car was made by Tipp & Co. Founded in 1912 in Nuremberg, Tipp & Co. was known for its large-scale tin-plate cars. 1930s; 20½in long.* **£800–£1,200**

▽ LIMOUSINE BY BING *The rear doors of this limousine by the German manufacturer Gebrüder Bing open. The car runs on a clockwork mechanism and has a driver. 1920s; 10½in long.* **£600–£900**

TIN-PLATE MOTORBUS

Patented by the German toy maker Ernst Lehmann in 1907, this 8-inch-long motorbus is a fine copy of a vehicle that was very common at the time. Its features include a uniformed driver and a staircase to the top deck; it is powered by a ratchet and spring mechanism. In excellent condition a bus like this is worth between £1,200 and £1,500.

▽▷ The ratchet and spring mechanism is visible when the bus is turned over.

▽ The dumbbell is the Lehmann trademark. The metal construction tabs can be seen beside the wheels.

△ Beneath the front, the axle, which is connected to the steering wheel, can be seen. Note that the tin has been marked "Lehmann".

German companies dominated both the production and export of tin-plate toys during the late 1800s and early 1900s. They even adapted their products to different countries using subtly varied colour schemes and lettering. The best German makers were Bing, Carette, Gunthermann, Märklin and Plank. As time passed, their dominance was challenged by British, French and American companies.

After World War I, British toy makers started to produce tin-plate pieces. The major names include Hornby (and Meccano which was made by Hornby), Lines Brothers (later Tri-ang), Chad Valley, Wells, Burnett and James Walker.

Tin-plate toys remained popular until the mid-1930s when the cheaper die-cast toys entered the market.

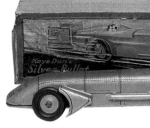

△ **KAYE DON'S SILVER BULLET**
Built to commemorate Kaye Don's attempt on the world land-speed record in 1930. It was made by the German firm Gunthermann in lithographed tin plate. 1930; 22in long. **£650–£850**

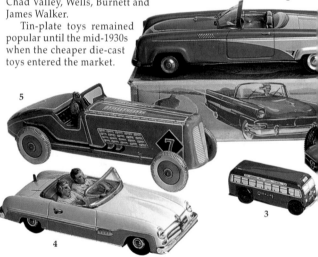

△ **GROUP OF TIN-PLATE CARS** *Even relatively modern mass-produced tin-plate vehicles can be valuable if in good condition; those that have been well used are often virtually worthless. Models that were produced in limited numbers also tend to be more valuable.*

1 *Open-top cruiser complete with box. c.1955; 13in long.* **£180–£250**. **2** *Racing car. c.1955; 9½in long.* **£120–£200**. **3** *Small bus. c.1955; 4½in long.* **£10–£15**. **4** *Open-top tourer. c.1955; 9in long.* **£80–£120**. **5** *Racing car. c.1935; 12in long.* **£80–£120**.

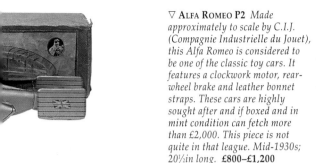

▽ **ALFA ROMEO P2** *Made approximately to scale by C.I.J. (Compagnie Industrielle du Jouet), this Alfa Romeo is considered to be one of the classic toy cars. It features a clockwork motor, rear-wheel brake and leather bonnet straps. These cars are highly sought after and if boxed and in mint condition can fetch more than £2,000. This piece is not quite in that league. Mid-1930s; 20½in long.* **£800–£1,200**

▽ **DISMOUNTING MOTORCYCLIST** *When wound up, the clockwork mechanism in this bike makes it travel along, stop to let the cyclist dismount and climb back on while the engine ticks over, and then continue on its way. Made by Arnold in Nuremberg, the MAC700, as it is known, is regarded as a classic of its type. 1950s; 6in long.* **£250–£350**

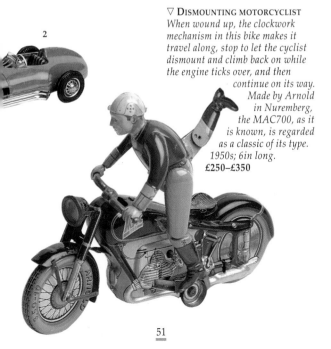

2

DIE-CAST VEHICLES

The appeal of die-cast vehicles, the most widely collected toys today in Britain, is due partly to the nostalgia collectors feel for the toys they played with when they were children and partly to the availability of such toys.

By the process of die-casting, huge numbers of cars, lorries and aeroplanes could be made inexpensively from a reusable mould. Various companies used slightly different materials for their toys, but most were lead based. They were finished in lead-based paints and could be produced far more cheaply than the lithographed tin-plate toys popular at the time.

To be of maximum value today, die-cast toys must be in perfect condition and still in their own original boxes.

In 1934, fired by the success of "Tootsietoys" from America in the early 1930s, the British Meccano company, part of the Hornby empire, pioneered its own range of die-cast model vehicles known as Dinky Toys. These were first intended simply as accessories to the successful O-gauge train sets Hornby was already making in quantity. Their popularity soon equalled that of the trains, however, and the company was quick to realize the value of these toys as playthings in their own right.

During World War II, toy production ceased, but by 1946 the Meccano company was again issuing a wide range of cars, vans, lorries, aeroplanes and ships. Some were reissues of old models, but many were new.

▽ RARE SET OF DINKY MECHANICAL "HORSES" *with detachable trailers in the liveries of the old British railway companies: maroon for the London, Midland and Scottish (LMS); brown and cream for the Great Western Railway (GWR); green for the Southern Railway (SR); and blue for the London and North Eastern Railway (LNER). c.1938; "Horse" and trailer 4½in long.* The set **£400–£600**

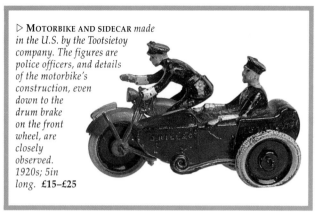

▷ **MOTORBIKE AND SIDECAR** *made in the U.S. by the Tootsietoy company. The figures are police officers, and details of the motorbike's construction, even down to the drum brake on the front wheel, are closely observed. 1920s; 5in long.* **£15–£25**

▽ **DINKY SUPERTOY LORRIES**
The perennial popularity of models of commercial vehicles of all types is reflected by this lorry, bearing the name of J. Lyons & Co., and the eight-wheeled, 14-ton Foden tanker. c.1955; Tanker 7¾in long. Lyons lorry **£400–£600**; Foden tanker **£100–£150**

△ **DINKY PLYMOUTH PLAZA**
This model of an American sports car (shown with its original box) was in production until 1963. c.1959; 4½in long. **£30–£40**

Dinky introduced a range of slightly larger models in 1948 known as Supertoys, into which most of the lorries and vans fell. As with the original Dinky Toys, it was the remarkable attention to detail and the high quality of the painting that put these vehicles ahead of most of the competition.

Since fewer models of the Supertoys were made than of the smaller range, some of these vehicles, for instance, eight-wheeled Foden lorries, are extremely rare and can command prices of £300–£400 when boxed and in good condition.

DATING DINKY TOYS

The following pointers give a general guide to dating, although there are exceptions.

Prewar Features

1 Plain metal wheel hubs.
2 Silver plating on wheels.
3 White tyres.
4 No model name and/or number on either the base plate or chassis.
5 Wing-mounted spare wheels.
6 Cars and lorries are boxed in sets, never individually.

Postwar Developments

1 Wheel hubs have a raised circle resembling a hubcap.
2 All models bear both a name and a number.
3 Dinky Supertoys were made only from 1947.
4 Windscreens from late 1950s.
5 Aluminium wheels date from 1959.
6 Opening doors and movable steering wheels etc. date from the early 1960s.

▷ **THREE DIE-CAST DINKY TOYS** *which are in excellent condition. The Foden flat truck is 8 inches long; the open-*

◁ **DINKY SUPERTOY TURNTABLE FIRE ESCAPE LORRIES** *such as these were first issued in 1958. The great discrepancy in the price of these two identical lorries demonstrates the importance to collectors of the condition of die-cast toys and the existence of the original box. c.1960; 6in long.*
Mint model **£150–£200**
Battered model **£2–£3**

topped sports car 3 inches long, and the Coventry Climax fork lift truck 6 inches long. All c.1955. The group **£180–£250**

After World War II, Dinky was challenged by other makers, notably Lesney, who in 1953 began to produce its Matchbox Miniatures – toys so tiny that they could often fit into a matchbox. These were mostly contemporary vehicles, but in 1956 Lesney launched the Models of Yesteryear range of larger classic vehicles and trains.

In the same year, the Mettoy company produced the innovative Corgi range of slightly larger vehicles, with windows, independent suspension and bonnets that could be opened to reveal the engine.

▽ **MATCHBOX REMOVALS VAN**
This flat-topped model, which was reissued in 1958 with a curved roof, was available in three other colours. c.1956; 2in long. **£35–£40**

△ **EARLY MATCHBOX CARS** *were distributed by Moko. Generally speaking, boxed vehicles are the most valuable, but here, the two-tone Vauxhall Cresta, although it*

△ **CORGI MGA** *The white-walled tyres on this die-cast sports car, with aluminium-painted hubcaps, are not accurate; they should be black. The car was also available with a cream or white body. c.1957; 4in long.* **£40–£60**

no longer has its original box, is the most sought-after model. 1950s; all vehicles 2in long. **£30–£40**

▽ **MATCHBOX "BROOKE BOND" TEA VAN** *Advertising on toy commercial vehicles, which proved popular with children, was first used in Britain by Hornby. 1950s; 2in long.* **£35–£40**

MODEL RAILWAYS

The first toy trains were made in the 1830s of either metal or wood and were pulled along the floor. It was not until later in the century that they were designed to run on tracks. By 1900, clockwork trains were common and the first electric sets had been invented.

Before World War I, the European market was dominated by German manufacturers such as Märklin, Bing and Carette. After the war, however, the field became more open. The English firm Bassett Lowke, which had distributed some of the German firms' products alongside its own, became more independent, and Hornby launched its first train set. In America, the important manufacturers were Ives, Lionel and American Flyer.

▽ PART OF A HORNBY TRAIN SET *with the original box behind. These clockwork O-gauge goods wagons are in excellent condition, which increases their value. c.1926; Large wagon 9in long.* **£100–£125**

▷ HORNBY "FLYING SCOTSMAN" *This locomotive came in a box with two carriages. The O-gauge range included models of many famous trains with the* correct colour schemes. c.1928; Locomotive 8in long. **£300–£500**

△ RARE ELECTRIC TRAIN SET
*Made by Ever Ready, this
unusual battery-operated
train set was part of a short-
lived attempt by the battery
makers to break into the toy*

*market. It is actually an
underground train set
with 1938 stock of London's
Bakerloo tube line. When new
it cost £3. 6s. 9d. c.1948;
Train 8in long.* **£100–£150**

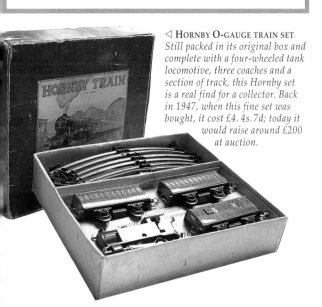

◁ HORNBY O-GAUGE TRAIN SET
*Still packed in its original box and
complete with a four-wheeled tank
locomotive, three coaches and a
section of track, this Hornby set
is a real find for a collector. Back
in 1947, when this fine set was
bought, it cost £4. 4s. 7d; today it
would raise around £200
at auction.*

Frank Hornby, the inventor of Meccano, was also one of the most influential model railway makers. In 1920, he launched his first train set with a simple clockwork tin train. His trains fitted track 1¼ inches apart, which was known as O gauge.

Over the next decades the variety of the toys increased and Hornby catalogues showed locomotives, tenders, carriages and accessories in a number of liveries. During 1925, Hornby produced its first electric train. It used the three-rail system, with an electrified central rail, and soon became popular.

The Dublo gauge, half the size of O gauge, was introduced in 1938. This range became famous around the world for the accuracy of detail, achieved using the die-casting technique, and the variety of locomotives, rolling stock and accessories.

△ **ELECTRIC LOCOMOTIVE**
Although this class 81 electric locomotive was made recently and so is relatively cheap to buy, its value will increase over the years making it a good potential purchase for new collectors. 1960s; 9in long.

▷ **THREE-RAIL ELECTRIC TRAIN**
Produced by Meccano, this goods train was part of the Hornby Dublo range. The middle rail of three-rail track was live and made electrical contact with a pick-up on the underside of the locomotive.

In 1938, Dublo, or OO, gauge was introduced to suit smaller houses. The width between the tracks was ⅝ inch, half that of the standard O gauge. c.1950; Engine 6in long. **The group £60–£80**

▷ **"SIR NIGEL GRESLEY"** *was the first model in the Dublo range introduced by Hornby in 1938 and it remains one of the most popular Dublo models. Pre-World War II examples can be identified by the deeper valance over the wheels. c.1950; 11in long.* **£150–£250**

HORNBY "PRINCESS ELIZABETH" LOCOMOTIVE

Probably the best-known model locomotive, the "Princess Elizabeth" was made in vast numbers. This 11-inch model, the Dublo version featuring the green livery of British Rail, was first issued in 1952.

Hornby released several versions of this locomotive. The most valuable is the larger O-gauge three-rail electric model launched in 1938 and decorated in the maroon livery of the London, Midland & Scottish Railway (LMS). Made in limited numbers, a boxed set in mint condition could fetch as much as £2,000.

This Dublo example dates from about 1958. **£60–£80**

CONSTRUCTION SETS

The first toys to be produced as construction kits were designed by Frank Hornby and based on gadgets he made for his sons. His first commercial toy, "Mechanics Made Easy", was a boxed collection of pierced metal components from which an endless variety of machines could be made. These sets, now rare, were renamed "Meccano" in 1907 and remained popular for more than 60 years.

Although successful, these kits did not produce lifelike cars or aeroplanes, which led Hornby in 1931 to introduce a range of constructor sets. With a simple nut and bolt assembly, beautiful toys could be built. These kits remained in production until World War II.

▽ **MECCANO SET** *complete with its original wooden box. This kit, no. 7, was the most comprehensive set available in the 1920s. Its range of plates, bolts and pulleys allowed complex pieces such as a loom to be built. c.1926; 26in wide.* **£600–£800**

◁ **RARE CONSTRUCTION SET**
*Complete with its original box
and instruction leaflet showing
the various models that could
be made from the kit, this
X-set was the smallest
kit available in the
Mechanics Made Easy
range. Dating from about
1906, the year before
these kits were renamed
"Meccano", it is rare
to find the complete kit
in good condition – a fact that is
reflected in its likely value at
auction. 12in long.* **£800–£1,200**

△ **"BLUEBIRD"**
*Made from Meccano, this model
is of Sir Malcolm Campbell's car,
"Bluebird", in which he repeatedly
broke the land-speed record during
the 1930s – most famously in 1935.
Streamlined models, such as this,
were only possible once flexible
metal construction plates had been
introduced, also in the 1930s.
c.1939; 22in long.* **£150–£200**

▷ **MECCANO SET NO. 7**
*In 1945, Meccano introduced
its famous red and green colour
scheme which remained in use
until the 1960s. Although this
set is in pristine condition, it is
much later than the other example
of set no. 7 featured here (above
left), hence the lower valuation.
c.1948; 19in wide.* **£150–£200**

GAMES

The appeal of games for
enthusiasts must lie partly in nostalgia
for childhood and partly in a delight
in the colourful diversity and
novelty of these toys.
The earliest commercially produced
board games were intended as
educational or moral aids for children,
but by the mid-19th century and early
20th century children played
games for fun alone.
At their most fascinating, board games
reflect the preoccupations of each age,
with subjects as diverse as military
battles, horse racing and space travel.
Others are bright new variations
of such age-old favourites as ludo
and snakes and ladders. Good examples
of collectable games can be bought for a
few pounds, while the most decorative
carved chess sets can command
thousands. Condition is all-important:
the most valuable games are those
that are undamaged and in the
maker's original box.

BOARD & OTHER GAMES

For over 5,000 years, board games have been played in all cultures. Traditional themes of confrontation, competition and chance still dominate new games today. Chess is one of the earliest "war" games, though the style of the pieces is medieval.

Victorian times saw a great expansion in board games, when favourites such as ludo and snakes and ladders emerged in the form children know today. The famous 20th-century game is Monopoly, which dates from the 1930s. Early sets can fetch hundreds of pounds.

The period feel of some games such as Cluedo and Dover Patrol, with its Dreadnought battle fleets, has a special appeal for collectors. Condition is all-important in assessing a board game's value, and many collectors never play their own games because of this.

△ VICTORIAN GAMES COMPENDIUM
Attractive set in mint condition containing both board and card games. The box is mounted with brass and inlaid with pietra dura *(semiprecious stone) plaques. Inside are ivory pieces for chess and backgammon, boards for cribbage and bridge, dice and turned wood shakers. Counters, shakers and cards are kept in the lower drawer (shown open here). c.1870; 14in wide.* **£1,200–£1,500**

◁ **ELECTRIC ROULETTE GAME** *made by Chad Valley. There are five coloured compartments in the box lid on which to bet. The wheel is spun and a metal ball drops through one of the holes around the tray causing a bulb to light in the winning compartment. c.1928; 14in x 10in.* **£25–£30**

△ **BONE AND BAMBOO MAHJONG SET** *in a wooden box. In this Chinese game, players try to win hands with combinations of tiles. 1920s; box 10in x 6in.* **£70–£100**

▽ **"THE INVASION OF EUROPE"** *A rare war game made by Chad Valley. Two rival invasion forces, one naval and one military, try to reach the ringed cities using dice and a compass (missing from this set). c.1910; 24in long.* **£80–£120**

△ **"MOTOR CHASE ACROSS LONDON"** *Geographica Ltd specialized in race games involving maps of Britain. 1930s; 20in long.* **£40–£60**

△ **VICTORIAN CHESS SET** The box, made from moulded composition on a cardboard support, is in the shape of a fortress, decorated with royal and courtly figures. It contains lead-weighted ebony and boxwood chessmen made by Jacques Staunton, the most celebrated designer of chess pieces. 1880s; 7in wide. **£800–£1,000**

▷ **CHESS SET** with large English barleycorn-pattern chessmen made of bone probably in India; one side is stained red. The overall quality is excellent and only the knights have needed repair. The fitted case is constructed of mahogany and is lined with velvet ribbon. 1825–50; 5½in wide. **£400–£600**

◁ **CHINESE CHESS SET** This high-quality set originates from Macau in southeast China. The chessmen are deeply carved and the set is complete with draughtsmen, dice and shakers. The box is of ivory inlaid in a form of pictorial marquetry known as intarsia. c.1860; 17in wide. **£1,000–£1,500**

△ **"PHYSOGS"** *An English game made by Waddy. Players are dealt a word that corresponds to a facial expression, such as "stubborn", and must accumulate cards, depicting eyes, nose, mouth and so on, which make up that expression when assembled. The winner is the player who comes closest to the ideal set by the makers of the game. 1930s; 14in x 10in.* **£30–£40**

▷ **TABLE-TOP HORSE RACING GAME** *made by Ayers and Co., makers of billiard tables. Based on roulette, it consists of a wheel with divisions that correspond to race horses with different odds. Bets are placed on the baize cloth before the "race", when the wheel is spun. c.1880; 5ft 8in long.* **£1,500–£1,800**

◁ **GERMAN SKITTLES SET** *comprising three geisha girls, three pug dogs (one with a crown), three tabby cats and a wooden ball. The skittles on turned wood bases are made of printed cloth, with metal-thread embroidery. c.1870; cat 7in high.* **£400–£500**

CARING FOR YOUR VALUABLES

ANTIQUES MAY BE BOUGHT FOR THEIR beauty, craftsmanship, history, rarity or even for their curiosity value. It does not matter whether you are buying an item because it gives you pleasure, or because you consider it to be a serious investment. It is important to see that it is well looked after and properly insured. That way, it can be enjoyed today and handed down from generation to generation.

As with any other collectable, precious dolls and toys require care and, sometimes, repair. But in many instances, it is better to leave teddies, rag dolls and soft toys in their original condition if you are considering selling them, since collectors often prefer to have any restoration work done themselves.

Bear in mind, also, that the best prices are achieved by pieces that have not undergone amateur restoration. So if you decide that the item needs mending, DIY repairs are seldom recommended. Poor-quality work often reduces the value of a doll, toy or game and can cause irreversible damage.

Experts always advise owners to seek out a first-class repairer or restorer. Even if their services seem rather expensive, it is cost effective to pay for excellent work by knowledgeable people.

Once your treasures are in good condition, help to keep them that way by following these tips.

CARING FOR TOYS

1 Keep dolls in a clean, dustproof box or case surrounded by acid-free tissue or card and away from any source of heat. If the doll is stuffed with hair or wool, it is wise to include a few mothballs from time to time, but do not let them touch the doll or its clothes.

2 Wooden dolls with gesso or varnished faces and limbs should never be cleaned with water, since both gesso and varnish are water soluble. The same applies to composition dolls. Both types can be cleaned with a soft brush or by rubbing with soft white bread.

3 Never attempt to clean or repair wax dolls; leave it to an expert.

4 Clean the faces of bisque or china dolls by wiping them with damp cottonwool with a little soap; wipe with another piece of damp cottonwool to remove the soap and dirt. Take care not to get the head or wig soaking wet. Allow to dry naturally.

5 Dolls sometimes need new wigs; do not use elaborate wigs made from nylon. Before deciding on a style, look at similar dolls to your own and decide what the wig should look like; replacement wigs can be expensive and hard to find. A new wig should be pasted on with a water-soluble glue.

6 Restringing limbs that have become detached, or restitching cloth or kid bodies, is best left to an expert.

7 Original clothing can enhance the value of a doll, but it needs to be treated with care. Any cleaning or mending is best done by an expert. Cloth is weakened every time it is cleaned, so don't clean it too often; never iron dirty fabrics, since heat may cause fading, fix stains and seal dust into the cloth.

8 Teddy bears, soft toys and rag dolls can be brushed and gently vacuumed to remove surface dirt. Occasionally they should be sealed in a plastic bag with insecticide pellets to prevent infestation by moths and other pests – but only if children are not going to play with the toy.

9 Dust tin-plate, brass, lead, cast-iron and die-cast toys gently with a soft brush or cloth. Remove any ingrained dirt with a non-abrasive silicone polish on a soft cloth. (Try it out on an unexposed part first.)

10 Never use abrasive cleaners on these toys, or polishes designed to revive the colour of full-size motor cars.

11 Don't repaint die-cast cars, for this will greatly lower their value.

12 Take batteries out of battery-driven toys when they are stored.

13 Oil moving parts of a clock-work mechanism with a drop of light oil. Wipe off any excess.

14 Where possible, save original boxes, but don't attempt to repair them yourself.

15 Periodically check wooden toys such as dolls' houses, Noah's arks and rocking horses for woodworm and treat them if necessary.

Insurance

The question of insurance is a matter of personal choice, and insurance companies vary greatly in the types of cover they provide – and the cost of the premiums. Cover for very valuable antiques can be expensive, but trying to find the lowest quotation is not necessarily the wisest course. Specialist brokers, as well as building society insurance services, understand the needs of collectors.

The first thing to do is to decide on the nature of the cover you require: the kind of "risks". Comprehensive and All In policies cover only certain specified perils, such as theft, fire, explosion, water damage or storm damage. In the event of theft, evidence will be required before a claim is met, and insurance companies will ask if the police have been notified.

Another type of cover is All Risks, which represents the maximum cover you are likely to obtain. It will also cover you against accidental breakage and disappearance, but not "inherent vice", such as the progressive deterioration of cloth-bodied dolls or dolls' clothes through atmospheric conditions.

Decide exactly what you want to insure and list the items with as much detail as possible. If your collection consists of a number of small items, such as toy cars, you may need to list them all. It is advisable to keep receipts as back-up evidence if you have to make a claim. Insurance companies also sometimes ask to see photographs, credit card vouchers or notes of any distinguishing marks.

You may even need to consider a policy that covers your possessions away from home, such as when they are sent to restorers or if you are selling them at an antiques fair.

VALUING YOUR POSSESSIONS

If you want to get a valuation of items you have inherited or had in your possession for some time, it is usually a good idea to obtain two quotes: from either reputable dealers or auction houses. (You may have to pay them a small percentage of the value.)

Most insurance valuations are based on the full market price, or replacement cost, of an item. That is why it is important to give your insurers as much detail as possible. For example, where the dolls, toys or games are kept and how they are protected. If you under-insure, insurance companies are likely to scale down their pay-outs – or may even refuse to pay out at all. It is now fairly standard practice for an insurer not to pay a claim in cash, but to settle the claim once you have bought a replacement. Frequently you are expected to pay an "excess", which can be, for example, the first £25 of the cost of each claim.

Index-linked policies automatically adjust the amount of insurance cover, and your premiums, every year. But it is still worth checking the figures from time to time. It is a good idea to have valuations updated every few years because fantastic appreciation often occurs with certain periods or pieces.

LOOKING AFTER YOUR ANTIQUES

Insurers are very keen that you take "reasonable" care of valuable items. Store dolls, toys and games at an even temperature in a dry place. Make sure that all shelves are strong enough to support the weight of the items that you place on them.

For instance, don't keep china dolls on a narrow, flimsy shelf or

wax dolls too close to a source of heat or where the sun might shine on them. If they get too warm, their eyes may protrude and the chemicals in their colouring may become purplish. Varnished dolls tend to yellow with age, and this will be accelerated by heat.

Don't keep toys and games directly under a water tank or bathroom.

It also makes sense to install smoke detectors, particularly in living areas, and to have fire extinguishers easily to hand.

If something does get broken or damaged, get the written approval of your insurance company before having it restored.

SECURITY

According to research, 1 in 12 households is burgled annually. But by joining a Neighbourhood Watch scheme, not only can the risk be reduced to 1 in 75, but you could also lower the cost of your home contents premium. The local Crime Prevention Officer will be happy to help you set up a scheme if none exists. Usually you need half the people in your area – whether it is a street or block of flats – to agree to join.

Normally your Crime Prevention Officer will also be happy to advise you if the locks and bolts on your house are adequate. Security devices such as five-lever mortise locks on doors and key-operated window locks are fairly inexpensive to fit and highly effective; they may even help to reduce the cost of your premiums.

As a rule, two mortise dead-locks should be fitted to each external door, and window locks to all ground-floor and first-floor windows. Vulnerable windows, such as those in a basement, should be fitted with iron bars. Additional precautions, such as security bolts on doors, are worth considering, especially where a door is not made of timber or is less than 1¾ inches thick.

Another way to deter burglars is to fit an alarm. This can also reduce your premiums, but don't go for the cheapest quote just to save a few pounds. You should choose a recognized organization that offers local maintenance facilities and a full guarantee. The local police or your insurers will probably be able to recommend appropriate companies to you.

If your home does get burgled, you should report the matter at the police station and to your insurers without delay.

National and Provincial Building Society, whose support helped to make this book possible, offers the insurance services the collector requires. Advice is available from its branches, or call Freefone 0800 80 80 80 for more details.

COLLECTOR'S CHECKLIST

PEOPLE ARE INSPIRED TO COLLECT toys and games for many different reasons: to form a collection or own a great rarity, for example, or even to acquire a plaything desired since childhood.

Movable models of human figures date back to the time of the Egyptians but, in collecting terms, the most desirable of the early dolls are the wooden ones that date from the 1600s. They are carved, covered in gesso (plaster mixed with size) and painted, and are often exquisitely dressed in contemporary costume. The best examples, in original condition, can fetch more than £30,000.

At the other end of the scale are the fabric and soft dolls made from the late 19th century. Fabric and rag dolls by companies such as Steiff, Lenci, Käthe Kruse, Norah Wellings and Dean's Rag Book Co. have become more popular over the last few years, with some examples made as recently as 1925 realizing more than £1,000.

The market for teddy bears has been buoyant for several years, but today all sorts of soft toys are enthusiastically collected, either by maker (such as Steiff, Dean's Rag Book Co., Merrythought or Schuco) or by type. Cartoon characters such as Mickey and Minnie Mouse, Donald Duck, Snow White and the Seven Dwarfs, Oswald Rabbit and Dismal Desmond are all popular.

The trains, boats and vehicles made from tin plate in the "Golden Age" of toy making, between 1900 and 1914, are most highly regarded in collecting circles, especially if they are by the best German manufacturers: Märklin, Bing, Gunthermann and Carette. Expensive when produced, these toys were the playthings of wealthy children; today the same toys can fetch tens of thousands of pounds if they are rare and in good condition.

Some collectors look for more modern battery-operated toys, including novelty figures, robots and space toys; and cars from the 1950s are extremely popular today. Toys that were made following the success of a film or television series, for example *Batman, Thunderbirds* or the James Bond films, have risen rapidly in price recently.

Condition is increasingly important with toys of this vintage, since collectors will only pay high prices for items in near mint condition with, if possible, their original boxes.

For many years, children's non-mechanical games and educational amusements were not as widely collected as clockwork toys, but there has been a great surge of interest, particularly in America, which has begun to affect prices in Europe.

The demand for board games, puzzles and educational toys reflects this new awareness, while the publication of specialist books has triggered wider interest in, for instance, pedal cars and rocking horses.

The number of collectors of toys and games continues to grow, and today the market thrives internationally, with regular auctions, fairs and exhibitions dedicated to the playthings from times past.

As with any other collectable, the best prices are achieved by items that have not undergone amateur restoration.

TIPS FOR BUYERS

1 Look at the back of a bisque doll's head for the maker's marks and the mould number. These enable the doll to be identified and valued.

2 Check the heads and limbs of china and bisque dolls for cracks or chips, since even a hairline crack will dramatically affect the value of the doll.

3 Look in the left ear of a soft doll or animal; if a small embossed metal rivet pierces the ear, it is likely to be a highly collectable product of the German manufacturer Steiff.

4 Check whether teddy bears or soft toys have been patched, darned or resewn – such repairs will adversely affect a toy's value.

5 Recently made dolls' prams have been imported into Europe from the Far East in vast numbers. Once "aged", they are difficult to tell from Victorian originals.

6 Many cast-iron mechanical money banks were copied and reproduced in Taiwan in the 1970s; these are worthless to collectors.

7 Check Hornby trains from the 1930s or Dinky Toys for metal fatigue. The alloy on some of these is prone to flaking and crumbling.

8 Don't buy rusty tin-plate toys. If they are badly affected, the decoration (and the toy) is likely to be unrestorable.

9 Playthings are worth more with their original boxes, but don't try to repair a damaged box yourself.

10 To be of interest to collectors, board games must be complete with their original playing pieces, dice and instructions.

SOME TOY AND DOLL MUSEUMS
Anglesey Museum of Childhood
1 Castle Street, Beaumaris
Gwynedd LL58 8AP
Telephone: 01248 810 448
Arundel Toy and Military Museum
23 High Street, Arundel
West Sussex BN18 9AD
Telephone: 01903 882 908
Bethnal Green Museum of Childhood
Cambridge Heath Road
London E2 9PA
Telephone: 0181 980 2415
Chester Toy & Doll Museum
13A Lower Bridge Street Row
Chester CH1 1RS
Telephone: 01244 346297
Haworth Museum of Childhood
117 Main Street, Haworth
Keighley, W Yorkshire BD22 8DP
Telephone: 01535 643593
Museum of Childhood Edinburgh
42 High Street (Royal Mile)
Edinburgh EH1 1TG
Telephone: 0131 225 2424
Ribchester Museum of Childhood
Church Street, Ribchester
Lancashire PR3 3YE
Telephone: 01254 878520

GLOSSARY

Note: SMALL CAPITALS within an entry refer to another entry.

A

"ALL BISQUE" DOLL Doll whose whole body is made from BISQUE.

B

BASSETT-LOWKE Company founded in Northampton in 1899 by W.J. Bassett-Lowke. Initially worked closely with BING and CARETTE, often importing German toy train parts into England. Established in its own right by the 1920s making model trains and boats, including some scale models.

BING Toy manufacturer founded by Adolf and Ignor Bing in the mid-1860s in Nuremberg. The firm made a wide range of boats, clockwork figures, steam-driven models, trains and cars. Bing toys were marked GBN (Gebrüder Bing, Nuremberg) until 1918 and BW (Bing Werke) after 1919. The Bing works closed in 1932.

BISQUE Unglazed biscuit porcelain used from the mid-19th C. After an initial firing, the doll's features were painted on. The porcelain was then fired at a low temperature to fix the colours.

BISQUE AND COMPOSITION DOLLS Dolls with BISQUE heads and COMPOSITION bodies.

BOULLE A form of MARQUETRY using brass and tortoiseshell INLAY, perfected in the 1700s by Louis XIV's cabinet maker André Charles Boulle.

BRITAIN, WILLIAM & SONS Founded in the mid-19th C in London, the firm later moved to Birmingham. During its early years, it made models, games and figures, but it only achieved fame after its move into hollow-cast lead figures in 1893. It is best known for its lead soldiers, although it also made farm and zoo sets and military items. In 1954 it acquired an interest in a local company of figure makers, Herald Miniatures. By 1959 the two firms had

fully merged and all products made were sold as Britains. W. Britains Ltd still exists today.

BUN FOOT Style of rounded, slightly flattened foot on furniture, used from the late 17th C.

C

CARETTE Company founded in 1886 by Frenchman George Carette in Nuremberg. Seen as one of the greatest toy manufacturers, it produced TIN-PLATE toys of the highest quality. The large-scale boats, cars and trains were hand enamelled. Carette had links with both BING and BASSETT-LOWKE. It closed in 1917 and did not reopen until after the end of World War I.

CELLULOID A type of plastic used for dolls as an alternative to BISQUE. It was given a flesh colour by adding pigment to the surface, which was then varnished.

CHAD VALLEY Joseph and Alfred Johnson founded this company in 1860 in the Chad Valley district of Birmingham. It moved to Harborne in 1897 and built up a reputation for well-made children's games. In the 1930s it began to develop and produce "low-quality" TIN-PLATE toys; it also made teddy bears and other soft toys. Between World War II and 1954 it produced DIE-CAST cars.

CODEG Trademark for toys such as the 1964 *Dr Who* Dalek (in both metal and plastic) and cheap TIN-PLATE toys that were distributed by the British company Cowan de Groot.

COMPOSITION PAPIER MÂCHÉ or wood pulp and glue, used for dolls' bodies from the Victorian period onward.

D

DIE-CASTING Process in which metal or plastic toys are produced inexpensively from a reusable mould.

DINKY TOYS Range of toys produced from 1933 by MECCANO.